RECORDED VERSIONS
GUITAR ®

AUTHENTIC TRANSCRIPTIONS
WITH NOTES AND TABLATURE

Transcribed by
KENN CHIPKIN
and
JACK MORER

SANTANA
GREATEST HITS

Cover photo by Ken Friedman

This publication is not for sale in
the E.C. and/or Australia
or New Zealand.

ISBN 0-7935-6409-3

HAL•LEONARD®
CORPORATION

7777 W. BLUEMOUND RD. P.O. BOX 13819 MILWAUKEE, WI 53213

SANTANA'S

GREATEST HITS

CARLOS SANTANA'S guitar work is among the most graceful and honest in rock. That this remains as true today as it did over 25 years ago, when his band burst onto the national scene as a highlight of the original Woodstock festival, comes as no surprise to fans of the electric guitar. From soaring melodies to throat ripping riffs, Carlos Santana's guitar work stands out in the crowd. Any crowd. Melodic grace, crying sustain and treacherous blues/rock solos have made him one of the electric guitar's most acclaimed and lyrical stylists.

Santana is also one of the few musicians who is just as eloquent speaking about his music as he is playing it. Carlos was a naturally insightful guide when asked to provide us with a tour of his greatest hits. Beyond anecdotal history, he revealed that some of his best-known moments of instrumental lyricisim actually had their roots in poems and lyrics. Having known Carlos for close to 20 years, this was news to me, but not a surpise from the man who claims Dionne Warwick and Aretha Franklin as influences on his six-string singing. Now using the "1812 Overture" to inspire "Soul Sacrifice" is another story – and one worth learning.

WHEN WAS THE FIRST TIME YOU HEARD "BLACK MAGIC WOMAN?"

It was in Fresno, California, at a soundcheck. Gregg Rolie brought the cassette in and said, "You'll really like this song." He wanted to know if we could try it. I remember I liked the way he (Peter Green in Fleetwood Mac) did it, but I didn't like it for us. He starts with a different kind of chord in the blues. Now when I listen to it I like it. But back then I said, "Let's do something different to it." So we started messing around with it and basically put more of a Calypso, African/Cuban thing on it.

BUT THE INSTRUMENTAL MELODY IN THE BEGINNING IS THE SAME.

The descending Wes Montgomery kind of melody is just basically "All Your Love" by Otis Rush. If you take the line "got a black magic woman" and put in the words "all your lovin' is lovin," you can hear that he changed the chords and made it so it's not ripping anybody off. It's like taking a seed and making a different tree with it, just like Luther Burbank used to do with Roses. He was a botanist who would crossbreed roses. The rose might be all white but just the tip would be red. Peter Green did something to it and we did something different to it. And people say, "Well it's got to be a Santana song." It's more Santana than Fleetwood Mac.

HOW DID "GYPSY QUEEN" GET GRAFTED ON THERE?

I'm pretty sure it was my idea to segue the two songs. At that time all I was playing was Gabor Szabo. I basically felt that I needed to escape from the B.B. King galaxy. Everybody, from Otis Rush to Buddy Guy to Mike Bloomfield to Peter Green, was playing B.B. King. So I needed to find my own thing away from B.B. I love him, but I felt like I needed to get out from under his spell. Gabor Szabo, Bola Sete, and Wes Montgomery got me out of it. I love the blues to this day. It's just that I didn't want to be an echo of somebody else. I wanted to find my own fingerprints. It's just like kids do today. You listen to this and that and by the time you sweat it, if you know how to do it, it comes out like you. Like Miles Davis. You can hear Billy Holliday and Louis Armstrong coming out of him.

DOES THE ORIGINAL "GYPSY QUEEN" BY GABOR SZABO SOUND AS SIMILAR AS "BLACK MAGIC WOMAN" DOES TO FLEETWOOD MAC?

No. Basically his is more acoustic with Ron Carter (bass). It's more subdued. Our "Gypsy Queen" has more of a Fleetwood Mac or Jimi Hendrix kind of energy.

IS THERE MORE TO THE ORIGINAL SONG THAN WHAT YOU PLAY?

Oh yeah, we played just little parts of it. In those days, they told us to edit everything. Originally we went to extremes. The first Santana band would play nothing but long jam songs. No bridge, no choruses, no intros, just long jams. Albert Gianquinto, who used to play piano with James Cotton, is the one who told us it would probably be better for our album if we just make songs 3 minutes long instead of 8 or 12 minutes long. So that's why we edited.

DO YOU REMEMBER AT WHAT POINT YOU STARTED TO DEVELOP YOUR SUSTAIN?

Way before I cut the first album. As soon as I heard "Supernatural" by Peter Green. Then there was Jimi Hendrix with "Foxy Lady" and Jeff Beck's *Truth* album. I said, "Oh!" Plus it came easy for me because I used to play the violin. Instead of using a bow, I just mark the floor where there is an umbilical chord happening between the guitar and the amplifier.

DO YOU USE A VIOLIN VIBRATO, WHICH IS MORE HORIZONTAL THAN UP AND DOWN?

I think so. It's more sideways, like Allan Holdsworth or Santo and Johnny. Don't laugh, man, that stuff sounds really good today. I love Santo and Johnny.

I LOVE THE SOUND OF IT AND THE SINGING QUALITY.

Yeah, that's what it is. Peter Green is the one that really did it for me. You should know "Supernatural," because that song is the most regal song you could ever hear on sustain. In fact, for anybody who plays with sustain, if they listen to that song, it makes all of us regroup. It's like learning how to tackle somebody. When you hear sustain like that you can tackle somebody, bring them down. You can bring their guard down so they have to listen to the whole song. It's an incredible song; it's on the *Hard Road* album with John Mayall.

OF ALL THE DIFFERENT "BLACK MAGIC WOMAN/GYPSY QUEENS" THAT YOU'VE RECORDED, DO YOU HAVE A FAVORITE RENDITION?

I'm partial to all of them. Some people say the first one. It sounds fine, but I think the way we're doing it now gets it over, otherwise I wouldn't be doing it.

MY FAVORITE RECORDING IS THE LIVE ONE ON THE VIVA SANTANA RECORD.

That was from a show in Montreal. That was a really good concert. Miles Davis said, "Sometimes there's one concert in 50 where you just show up and it all happens. You don't have to do anything." I think that was one of those concerts.

"EVERYBODY IS EVERYTHING" IS A DEPARTURE FOR YOU. IT'S A ROCK SONG.

It's a combination of what was happening in San Francisco with Tower of Power and Santana. It's a mixing pot of Afro-Cuban and Tower of Power funk. I used to picture Aretha Franklin singing it. The message is get into the new millennium, which is what everybody is talking about. If you listen to the lyrics, it talks about something that we are relating to today; a new day come around. I wrote the lyrics because I didn't like the original ones, which were just about karate before Bruce Lee. It was a karate song. I called the guys in the Emperors and asked if it was okay to use the music to their song "Karate," but change the lyrics. They said, "Do what you want." As long as they get the royalty, there was no problem.

YOUR TAKE ON IT WAS MORE LIKE ERIC CLAPTON.

That's because it's not me. 75 to 80% of it is Neal Schon. I don't play like that. You're right, it's basically an Eric Clapton kind of thing from *Derek and the Dominos*, which Neal was listening to a lot. In fact I think they called Neal the Eric Clapton of the Bay Area.

WHY DID YOU WANT A SECOND GUITAR PLAYER?

Because I heard a voice. It's the same question Miles Davis asked me. Miles never liked another guitar player in the band. So he was always on my case, "Why did you get that mutherfucker?" I just hear another sound. Plus, I don't have a big ego like a lot of people. I don't care whether it is Sonny Sharrock or Jeff Beck. If I hear a sound I go for it.

WHERE IS THE BEST NEAL SCHON? WAS IT ON A SANTANA RECORD?

Probably that "Everybody is Everything" and "Song of the Wind," which we did as half and half. We both traded off a lot.

ON "SONG OF THE WIND" I STILL CAN'T HEAR WHERE ONE OF YOU LEAVES OFF AND THE OTHER TAKES OVER.

Well by that time he was coming more to my side. I wasn't going to go to his side, which is Eric Clapton. I love Eric Clapton and B.B. King, but I'm always looking to find my own fingerprints. You can trace me more to Gabor Szabo and singers. I used to sing "Never Gonna Give you Up" by George Butler, the original Ice Man. I used to listen to a lot of singers. Vernon Reid and I discussed how we listened a lot to Dionne Warwick. That's where we learned how to sing. She has a very beautiful middle path where she doesn't sound black or white. She just sounds like a soul. Like a glass of water with no color in it. I like that tone, I like that sound.

"SONG OF THE WIND" SOUNDS LIKE A COMPOSED SOLO. DID YOU WRITE IT OUT OR DID YOU REHEARSE IT AHEAD OF TIME?

No, Gregg Rolie and I started playing two chords, the same chords we used on "Incident at Neshabur" and everything else that I use , F to C (Fmaj7 to Cmaj7), and I just went a different kind of way. Then I started putting in all the things that I was listening to at that time, like "Love on a Two Way Street." When you listen to all those songs on *Caravanserai*, you can hear everything I used to listen to then from *Sketches of Spain* by Miles, to *First Light* by Freddie Hubbard. "Song of the Wind" is a melody and an improvisation. Basically, I would stick to a theme. That's the thread to dance around. Once you go out, then I'll find another thread. He'll find one and then I'll find one. It was kind of like running a relay with a baton. He passed it to me, and I was passing it to him.

FMAJ7 TO CMAJ7 RESONATE WITH YOU. WHAT DO THEY GIVE YOU?

To me it's like the Grand Canyon. You can never see the Grand Canyon the same way twice. It's always different. Within those two chords you could put "Fool on the Hill" by the Beatles and a million other songs and they all fit. It's the closest thing to that universal corridor when everything can be played.

NEAL MUST HAVE BEEN USING A LES PAUL ON "SONG OF THE WIND."

We both bought them at the same time. They looked like identical sunbursts. His got ripped off and I gave mine to Mr. Udo, who is the greatest promoter in Japan.

WHAT KIND OF AMP WERE YOU USING FOR *CARAVANSERAI*?

Straight ahead two Fender Twins.

DID YOU HAVE AMP SETTINGS YOU STARTED WITH?

Just anything and everything to sustain without the pedals. I never like sustaining pedals.

WHAT WAS YOUR EQUIPMENT SETUP FOR *ABRAXAS*?

Pretty much Fender Twins and a Les Paul guitar.

WHAT WAS IT LIKE RECORDING *SANTANA* AND *ABRAXAS*?

Abraxas was all done very quickly at Wally Heiders Studio in San Francisco by Fred Catero. We were already doing the songs live. That was the good thing about the first band and album. Everything that we played we were already playing live, so by the time we went to the studio, we knew it. We were playing it almost like a year or something like that before we recorded most of those songs. That was basically the seeds of the first album. I remember we were in Boston, in Cambridge, walking around a week or two weeks before Woodstock, when it came out. Oh man! We liked the songs but we just hated the sound. Everything sounded kind of thin. It got messed up in the mastering.

THE WHOLE RECORD WAS DONE WITH A GIBSON AND THE FENDER TWIN AMPS.

The first one was pretty much done with the red Gibson SG you saw at Woodstock. The second one and third one and *Caravanserai* was with the Les Paul and always the Fender Twins. Not until the middle part of *Caravanserai* did I discover the Boogie amp. The Boogie came through with an extra knob for sustain, which was my idea. I said, "Can you add an extra knob so I can crank the first one to 10 and sustain, and bring the other one to 3 so it's not so loud?"

YOU WERE THE MASTER VOLUME MAN FOR BOOGIE?

To my recollection, I'm the one that suggested it to him, if he could do such a thing. To my surprise, he did it and he blew me away. It was just necessity. I don't know anything about ohms except chanting it! Other than that, I don't know nothing about wire. But I did know that it made sense to me that if you added a master volume that you could use one to control the actual volume and the other one to control the intensity of the sustain.

TELL ME ABOUT "EVERYTHING IS COMING OUR WAY"

To me, the greatest poets America has are Bob Dylan, Smokey Robinson and Curtis Mayfield; that's strictly a Curtis Mayfield kind of song. I started to hear different kinds of chords that were getting me ready for *Caravanserai* and all the other stuff with Stanley Clarke. I was getting ready to do something different than eating the same thing for breakfast every morning.

WHAT IS THE STORY BEHIND "EVIL WAYS?"

It's a Sonny Henry song by way of Willie Bobo. Bill Graham used to have a thing with Tito Puente and Willie Bobo and all those guys. He told Willie Bobo, "There's a band from San Francisco and I'm going to give them 'Evil Ways,' and they are going to take it further than you did." So he invited us to his office and he just played it for us. At first, it sounded a little foreign to us but once we played it, it was so natural. Like "Black Magic Woman." Some things just fit you so naturally. Thank you Bill Graham.

IT'S ALSO GM TO C, WHICH IS A VERY COMFORTABLE AREA FOR YOU.

It's pretty much like the Carole King thing, "It's Too Late," and all those songs which people were playing a lot in those days.

WAS "EVIL WAYS" RECORDED QUICKLY?

Yeah, that was recorded really quickly. That was the first album. The first album was done with everything within less then a week. I think in 3 days it was recorded and mixed. We didn't know that we could take our time and get better sounds with it. So everything was kind of rushed. We had opened enough times for Paul Butterfield and Creedence Clearwater Revival and everybody playing those songs that we really did know them. We didn't know about taking our time with the board and getting a better sound. I think we did the best with what we knew, what we had.

"I HOPE YOU'RE FEELING BETTER?"

It's a Gregg Rolie song. That's when I used a Marshall for the first time. That's a Gregg Rolie song, a Gregg Rolie approach. That's what he heard. You want me to go through a Marshall, cool. Crank it up, cool. "Mother's Daughter" is another Gregg Rolie song.

"INCIDENT AT NESHABUR" HAS ALWAYS BEEN AN IMPORTANT SONG FOR YOU.

I'm really fond of that song. It's got the same chord progression at the end of it as "Song of the Wind." The first part on the piano is kind of like Horace Silver. There were no lyrics but it was a pimp poem we chanted that ended the line with "Go ahead brother right on." It was a street slang thing.

Gregg Rolie (Vocals, Keyboards)

photo by Ken Friedman

YOU CHANTED IT IN THE STUDIO WHILE YOU WERE RECORDING THE OPENING CHORDS TO "INCIDENT?"

Yeah, that was an Albert Gianquinto thing. That was his intro and the second half was my part, where it slows down. We worked it out. I needed to go to that transition so when we slow it down, we put a kind of waltz-like descending line to get us into that progression of C into the F.

YOU AND JEFF BECK ARE SO MELODIC.

Jeff is a great player. He is somebody that can really give life to a tune. The other one is Eric Johnson. I'm waiting for him to play more songs. He is a very melodic cat. That's the whole thing, melodic and lyrical, like Miles.

"JINGO (JI-GO-LO-BA)" IS A STANDARD.

It's an Olatunji song in B minor.

HOW WERE YOU INTRODUCED TO IT?

Carlos Santana (Lead Guitar, Vocals)

By walking through Aquatic Park in San Francisco, where they have a bunch of conga players and people smoking pot and drinking wine and watching the ladies go by and playing blues. They always sang that song. Again, we put a guitar in there and the bass line. We did something different to it so it would sound different then Olatunji or the way the guys at the fountain in New York at Central Park or Aquatic Park do it. They still play that song if you go there. It's a very masculine song. Olatunjui's album was called *Drums of Passion*. It's very sensual.

"OYE COMO VA?"

Is definitely something that I heard late at night. I knew without a shadow of a doubt that "Oye Como Va" was a party song. When you play it people are going to get up and dance. That's what it is, a party song like "Louie Louie."

TELL ME ABOUT "PERSUASION."

It's burning with funk. It was kind of like where Vernon Reid was going, more rock, almost like punk rock. The energy is very primitive.

photo by Jeffrey Mayer

"SAMBA PA TI" IS A SPECIAL SONG FOR YOU. YOU NAILED THAT ONE.

Jose "Chepito" Areas (Percussion)

photo by Ken Friedman

"Samba Pa Ti" is something that I wrote in New York City. We had just gotten back from our first trip to Europe and I had serious jet lag. When you are weak like that from jet lag, good things come in and bad things come in and out. You've got to be really careful. I was in a very fragile receptive mood. I heard this guy playing a saxophone outside of my window. He was trying to play bebop. After a while I looked out the window to see what it was and it was this guy who looked like he just got off a merry-go-round that was going 1,000 mph, so he couldn't stand up straight. You could tell the whole world was moving too fast on him. He was nodding back and forth. It broke my heart because he looked like me and he looked like everybody, every man that I know, in the sense that he didn't know what to put in his mouth: The bottle of booze from his pocket or the saxophone's mouthpiece to play. His mind couldn't decide. He would put the sax almost to his lips and then he put it out and he grabbed the bottle. He almost took a drink. He was moving around like he was dizzy. It just broke my heart. Because when I saw him I saw all of us battling on this planet. Because we are all doing time on this planet. So what I heard first was the poem. The poem went through every step in life you find, freedom from within. Freedom comes from within. So "Samba Pa Ti" is a way to get people out of that headlock from a demonic force. A demonic force is what makes a man be lost like that. So when I wrote the poem it went "through every step in life you find," it was a melody that was put to this poem. When I played it I showed it to the guys and some of them said that's nice. When we went to record it, people didn't want to do it. To my recollection, that was the first time I actually pulled rank on the band and said this song goes in or I'm out, get somebody else kind of thing. I had to fight for it. Finally when everybody said, "Well you put it that way, I guess it's going to go." Once we did it, it was one take. Gregg and I. I'm really glad I did it because I hear a lot of people doing it like Ottmar Liebert. There's a story in there. You don't always have to have words in English or in Spanish. You can say a whole song just like "Europa" or "Samba Pa Ti" from beginning to end and it's a straight ahead melody thing, which now I hear Steve Vai is doing.

DO YOU HAVE A COMPLETE SET OF LYRICS TO "SAMBA PA TI?"

Basically it goes, "Through every step in life you find freedom from within, and if your mind should understand, woman love your man. Because everybody is searching for eternal peace. It is there, all you have to do is share." Those are the lyrics. I don't want anybody to sing it.

THERE IS ONE MOMENT IN THERE THAT IS CLASSIC. IT'S WHERE YOU SWITCH PICKUPS. IT'S A BONE CHILLER (25TH BAR, WHERE IT SAYS RAKE).

That's in the G to Am part. I did it because the treble pickup is like the alto or the soprano. The bass pickup is like a tenor. Once I couldn't hear anymore of that tenor tone, I just switched to the alto or the soprano, which is the more female. Treble is female, and, of course, bass is masculine. That's the way I always look at it. When I finished the solo the headphones were on my forehead and the back of my head instead of on my ears. I was bobbing and weaving and trying to complete the song without stopping, because it came in as one stream. I remember the first thing I asked everybody was "How was that?" I had no idea, man. It's like riding a black horse with no saddle. You just try to stay on it, which is really what it is, riding a solo. For an emotional solo, you've got to stay on it even if you think you fall off. I always look at it that way.

"TOUSSAINT L'OVERTURE" IS A JAMMING SONG.

Toussaint was the guy who defeated Napoleon before Waterloo. He was a black man who kicked Napoleon's butt. We wrote it for him. It is basically the same chorus.....

AS "WALK DON'T RUN"....

And "California Dreaming," and "Hit the Road, Jack." It's the same chords. Those chords are, again, like a big old tunnel that a lot of songs can fit through.

IT WAS HARD FOR ME TO TELL IF IT WAS A PROGRESSION YOU JAMMED ON OR A MELODY SONG.

Michael Shrieve (Drums)

photo by Ken Friedman

We always jam. But whatever we jam, there was always some kind of theme in it. That's the first thing that people told me when I started in Haight Ashbury. "Man, you are different. You are very melodic, very lyrical even though you are just jamming." They said, "We know that you don't know what you're doing, but its very lyrical." No matter how crazy things get, I always have to hear Aretha or Dionne Warwick singing in there. That's what keeps me melodic or thematic. Otherwise it just sounds like a bunch of notes and you lose me. You also lose the people.

WHAT WAS THE SEED FOR "SOUL SACRIFICE?"

It came from this conga player named Marcus Malone, and also from Aquatic Park where all the conga players hang out. Basically, he had a riff, and Gregg and I had another riff, and we were thinking more symphonic. We were listening to the "1812 Overture" a lot in those days. We would take acid and we used to play that to clean the house. You know hippies can get funky after a week. That was the only time I ever played classical music, when we hippies wanted to clean the house. Anything else wouldn't work because we just wouldn't clean the house. We'd just started tripping. We wouldn't start cleaning the house until we started listening to this classical music. Think the main melody to the "1812 Overture." Then, put in the rhythm guitar/organ part of "Soul Sacrifice;" yeah, that makes sense. It was the closest thing we ever got to European classical music.

WHAT'S THE STORY BEHIND "WINNING?"

That came from Bill Graham. Nona Hendryx from LaBelle did it first. I play a Stratocaster through a Boogie. I think my tone sounds like the guy from Dire Straits (Mark Knopfler). It's nice to play a Strat once in a while, although I don't lean on it as much because you have to play so loud. Stevie Ray or Jeff Beck or Jimi had to play so loud to get a tone. I don't like to play that loud if I can help it, because I don't like the extremes. Some guys play really loud for a year and then the next years they play acoustic music and they don't want to hear anything. I avoid those extremes. That's why I don't play a Strat. Once I find an amplifier that can sustain the way I want to with the tone that I want, then I'll switch to the Strat.

SO IT WAS A CONSCIOUS DECISION TO CHANGE YOUR TONE ON THAT SONG?

Yeah it was. I was playing a Strat a lot at home and I noticed that it had that sweet sound. Everybody calls it the candy sound, because with the single-coil pickups, you get a sweet candy sound.

YOU NEVER PLAYED THAT SONG MUCH LIVE.

That's true. It was the time when I was hanging out with certain people in L.A., and I don't hang out with those people in L.A. anymore. It's kind of like an L.A. song. I'm not into L.A. rock anymore.

IS THERE ANYTHING YOU WANT TO SAY ABOUT PERFORMING THESE SONGS LIVE?

You have to feel it. If you don't feel it, nobody is going to feel it. It don't matter whether you are playing "La Cucaracha," "A Love Supreme," or "Beethoven's 5th" or "9th," if you don't feel it, nobody is going to feel it. You have to be conscious of what you play. There is something that goes beyond the note and the chord. You have to be able to feel it. Otherwise other people are not going to feel it.

Armando Peraza (congas, bongos, percussion)

photo by Jeffrey Mayer

Black Magic Woman

Words and Music by Peter Green

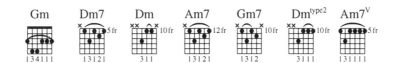

Intro
Moderate Latin ♩ = 120

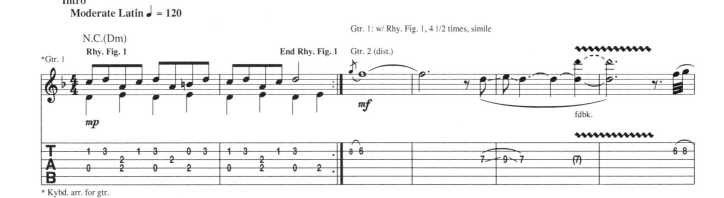

* Kybd. arr. for gtr.

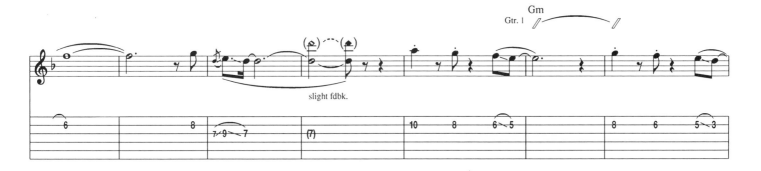

slight fdbk.

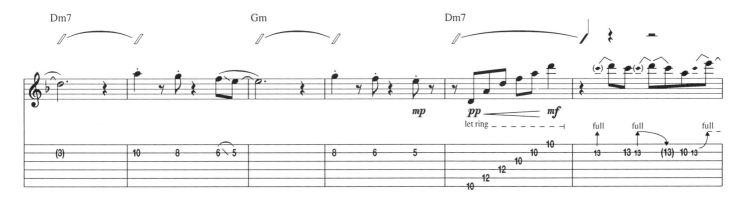

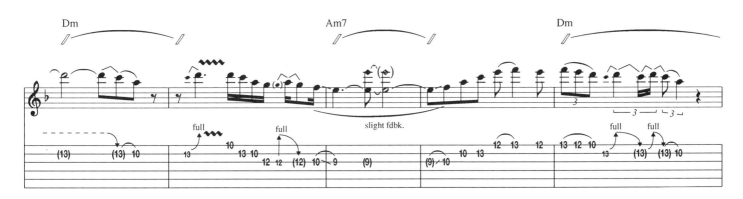

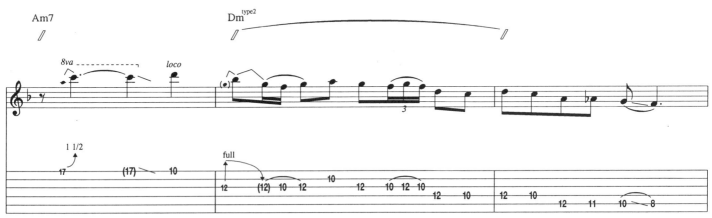

Verse

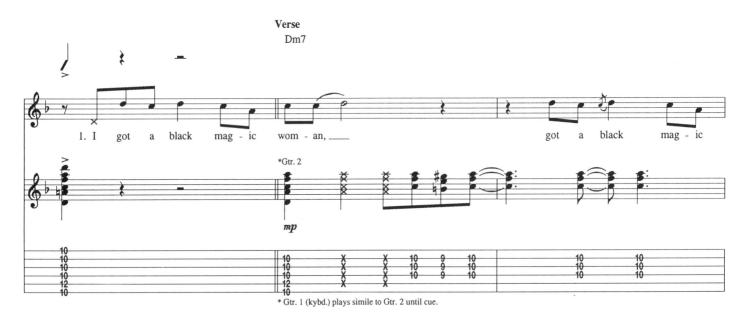

1. I got a black mag - ic wom - an, ___ got a black mag - ic

* Gtr. 1 (kybd.) plays simile to Gtr. 2 until cue.

wom - an. ___ I've got a black mag - ic wom - an,

Gm

stop mess-in' 'round _ with your _ tricks. ___ Don't turn your

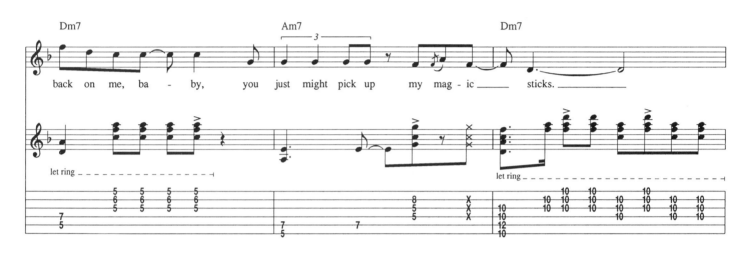

Dm7   Am7   Dm7

back on me, ba — by, you just might pick up my mag-ic ___ sticks. ___

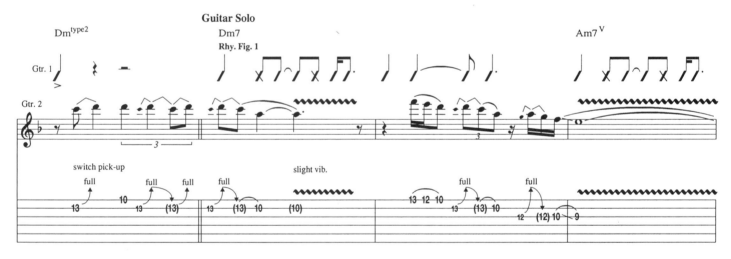

Guitar Solo

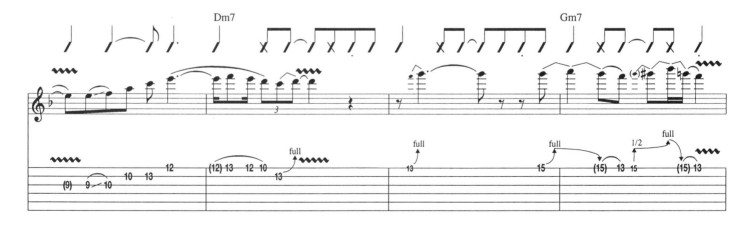

me, ba - by. Yes, ___ you got your spell on me, ba - by,

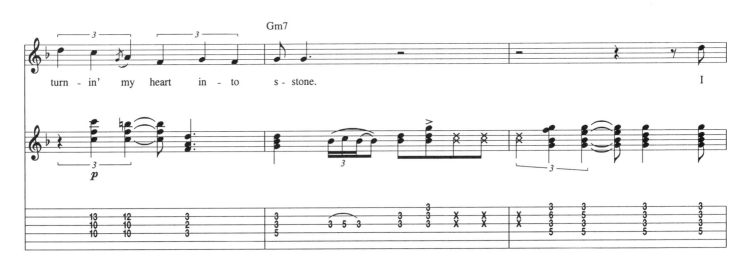

turn - in' my heart in - to s-stone. I

need you so bad, ___ mag - ic ___ wom - an, I can't ___ leave you ___ a - lone. ___

Outro   *Fade Out*

Gtr. 1: w/ Rhy. Fig. 1, simile, till fade

N.C.(Dm)

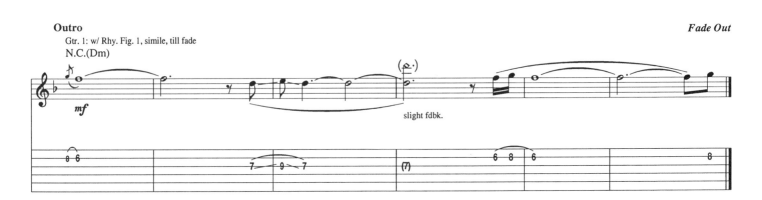

slight fdbk.

Everybody's Everything

Words by Carlos Santana
Music by Tyrone Moss and Milton Brown

20

your light might shine in this whole town.
(This whole town, this whole town, this whole town.)

Sing it loud, time for you to all get down.
(Yeah do it, yeah)

Organ Solo

Get

Gtr. 2

Riff B

End Riff B

read - y, uh! Get uh! Dig this

D.S. al Coda

sound, it's been a - round and round and round.
(Yeah, do it.)
4. Could you

$\oplus$ *Coda*

Guitar Solo

(Yeah, do it.)

Gtr. 3 (dist.)

8va

full full full full 1/2

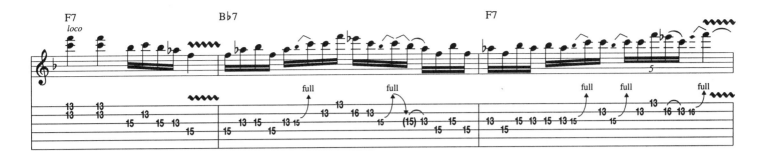

Gtr. 2: w/ Riff C, 3 times, simile

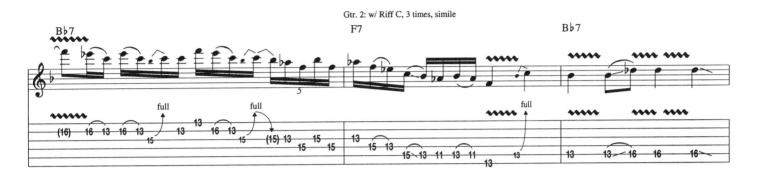

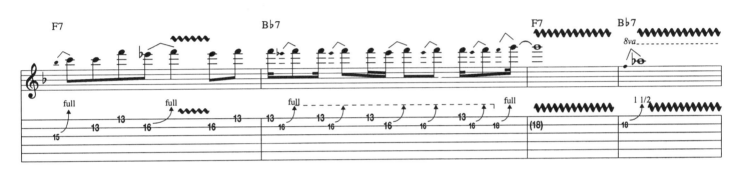

Gtr. 2: w/ Riff B

Gtr. 1: w/ Riff A, last 2 meas.

Uh!   Sing   it   loud,   time for you to all __ get

Outro

Play 6 Times & Fade

Gtr. 3 tacet
Gtrs. 1 & 2: w/ Rhy. Fig. 1

down. __

(Yeah, do it.)

Everything's Coming Our Way

Words and Music by Carlos Santana

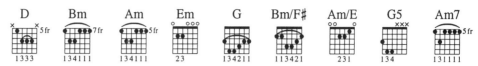

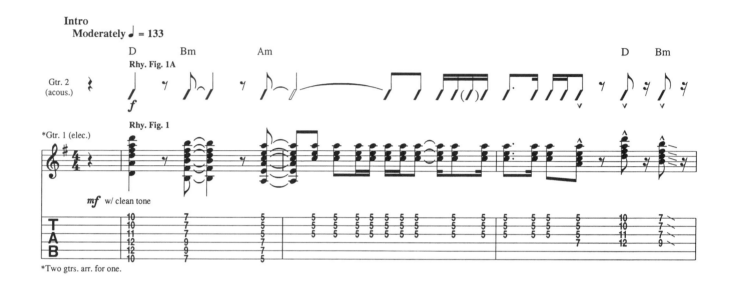

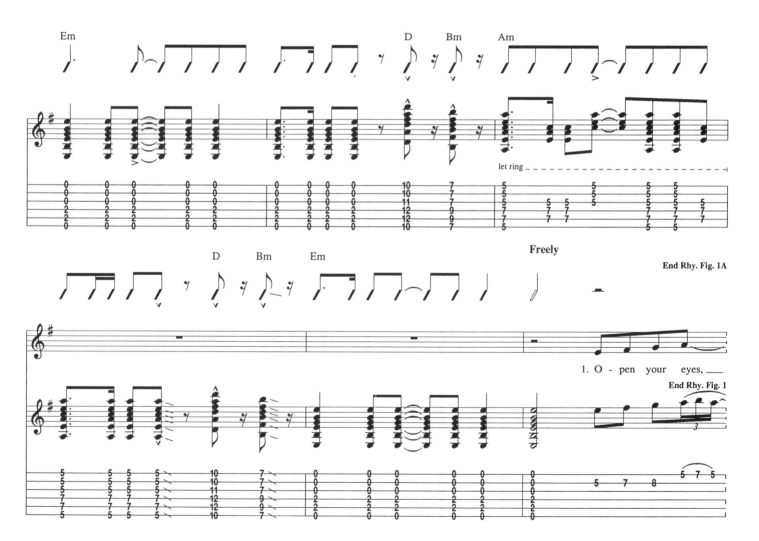

Evil Ways

Words and Music by Sonny Henry

%S **Verse**

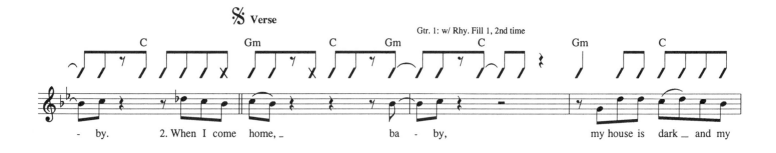

- by.   2. When I come home, _ ba - by,   my house is dark _ and my

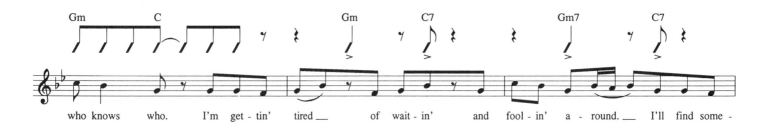

thoughts are cold. _ You hang a - round, _ ba - by,   with Gene and Joan _ and a -

who knows who.   I'm get - tin' tired _ of wait - in'   and fool - in' a - round. _ I'll find some -

To Coda ⊕

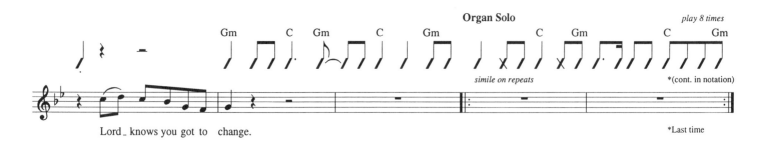

bod - y   that won't make   me feel like a clown. _ This can't go   on.

Organ Solo   *play 8 times*

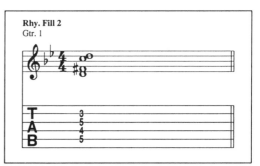

Lord _ knows you got to change.   *Last time*

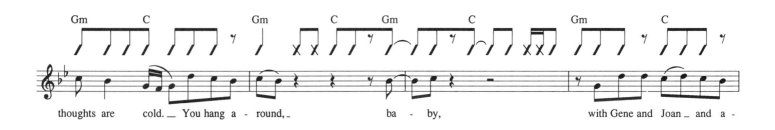

Rhy. Fill 1
Gtr. 1

Rhy. Fill 2
Gtr. 1

Gypsy Queen

Words and Music by Gabor Szabo

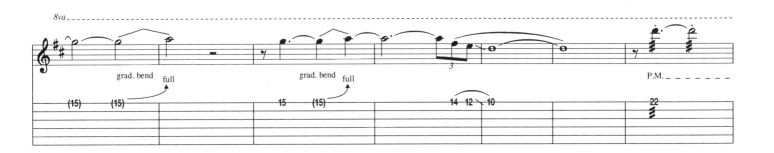

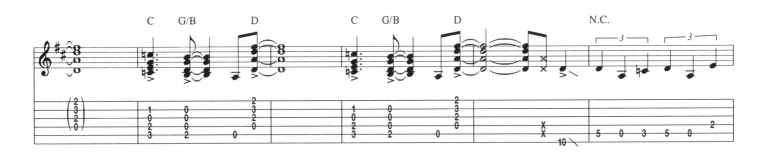

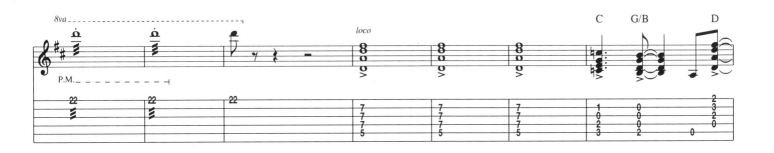

pitch: C#

Hope You're Feeling Better

Words and Music by Gregg Rolie

*Key signature denotes E Dorian. **Chord symbols reflect overall tonality.

Well, / I hope you're feel - in' bet-ter.
And, \ I hope you're feel - in' bet-ter.

Yes, I hope you're feel - in'

search-in' for a good time?
wait-in' for the sun - shine?
mov-in' to a new town?

Is that you,
Is that you,
Is that you,

wait - ing for all these years?
when all you see is clouds?
Well, that won't re-place your pen-ance.

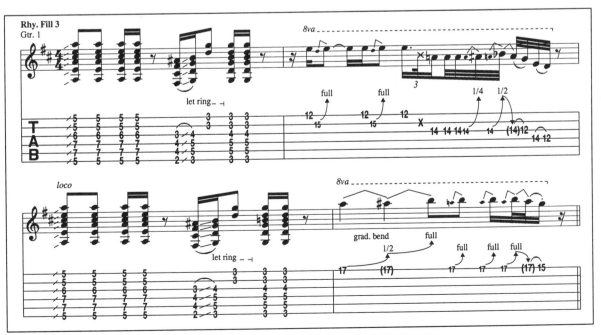

Outro Guitar Solo
Double-Time Feel

Em

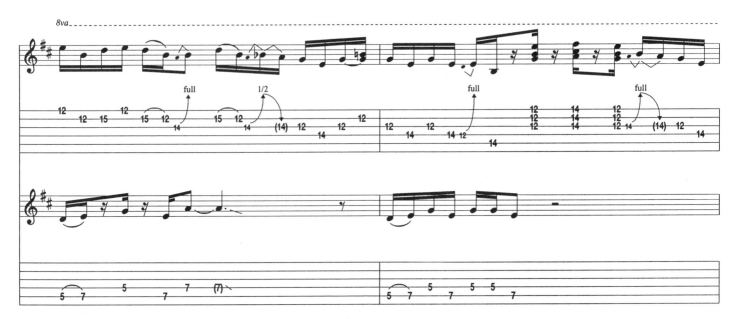

Incident at Neshabur

Words and Music by Albert Gianquinto and Carlos Santana

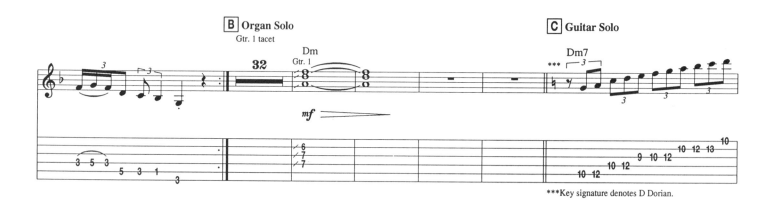

*** Key signature denotes D Dorian.

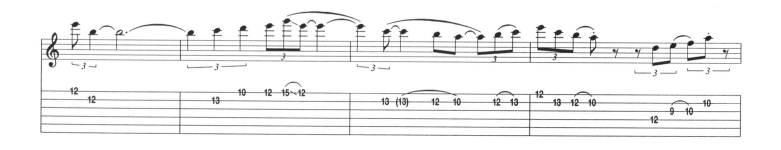

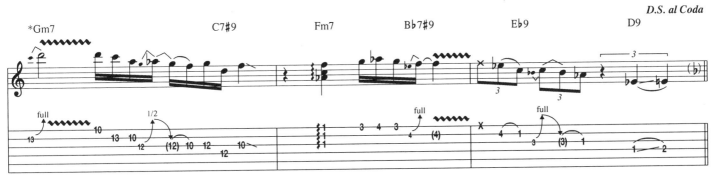

D.S. al Coda

* Chord symbols derived from piano.

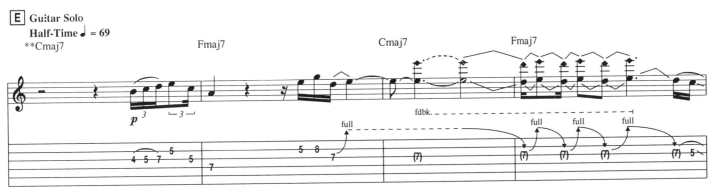

** Chord symbols derived from organ.

Jingo (Ji-Go-Lo-Ba)

Words and Music by Michael Olatunji

Mother's Daughter

Words and Music by Gregg Rolie

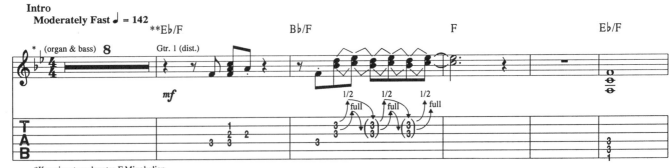

Intro
Moderately Fast ♩ = 142

*Key signature denotes F Mixolydian.

**Chord symbols reflect overall tonality.

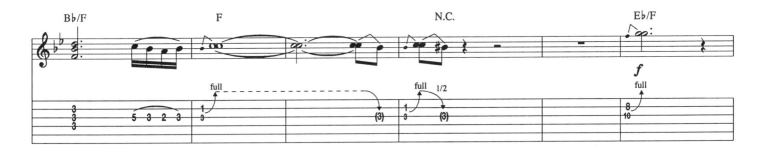

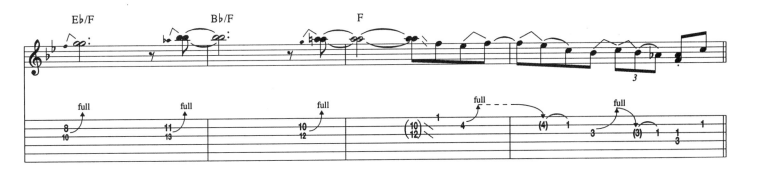

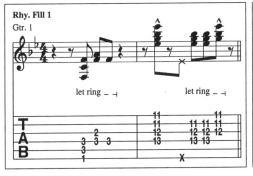

You — played it out, thought you had it made. —
I got to — leave — 'fore I get much — old - er,
I got — some - one to — take — you o - ver,

and it looks like some - one passed you by _____ a - gain. —
'cause she ain't moved_ in near - ly for - ty days. _____
your _ moth - er ain't so proud, what hap-pened to you. _____

Hey, _____ yeah, _

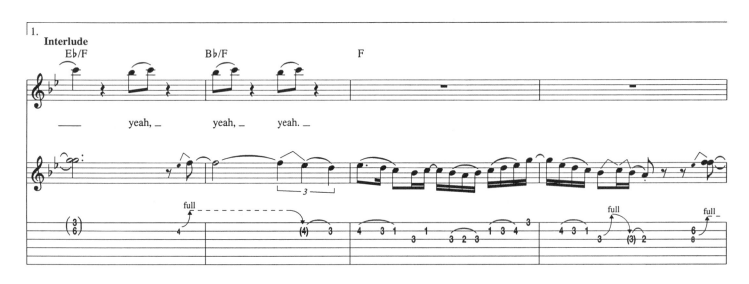

1.

Interlude

— yeah, _ yeah, _ yeah.

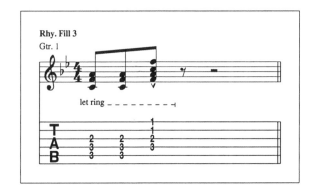

48

*Switch to bridge pickup.

Outro Guitar Solo

** Key signature denotes G Mixolydian.

Oye Como Va

Words and Music by Tito Puente

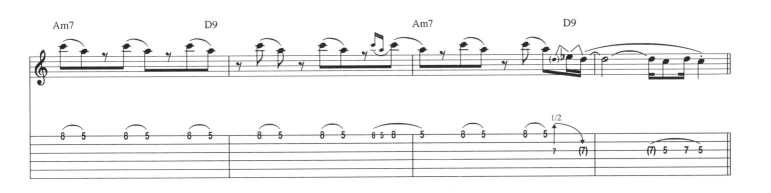

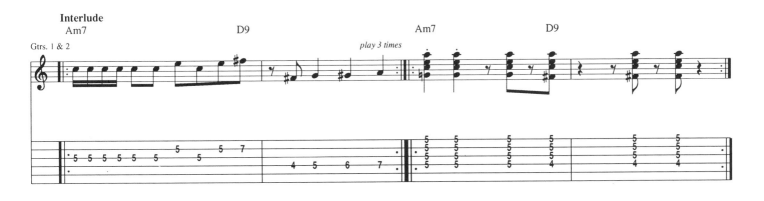

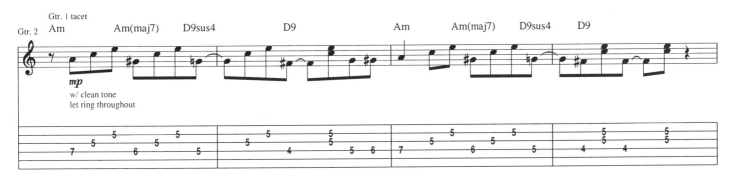

Am7 Am(maj7) D9sus4   D9   Am   Am(maj7) Am7   Am6

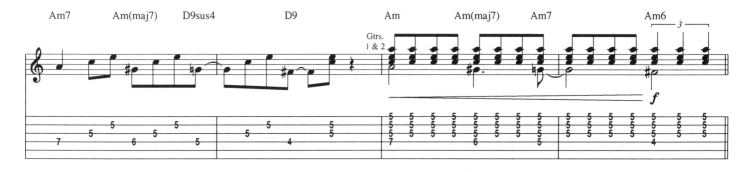

Organic Solo
Gtr. 2: w/ Rhy. Fig. 1, 11 times, simile

Bridge
Gtrs. 1 & 2: w/ Rhy. Fig. 1, 2 times

               Am   D Am

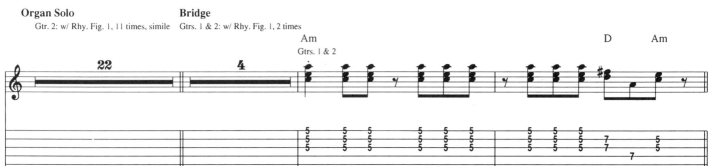

Verse
Gtrs. 1 & 2: w/ Rhy. Fig. 1, 2 times, simile

Am7   D9   Am7   D9

Oy - e co - mo va,   mi rit - mo. Bue - no pa go - zar,   mu - la - ta.

Bridge

D7
Gtrs. 1 & 2

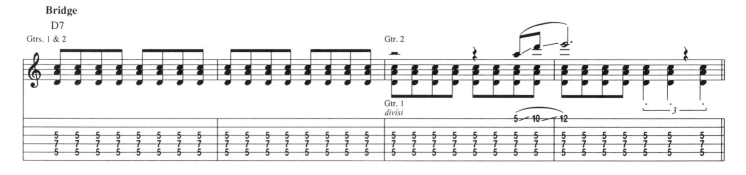

Guitar Solo
Gtr. 1: w/ Rhy. Fig. 1, 12 times, simile

Am7   D9   Am7   D9
Gtr. 2

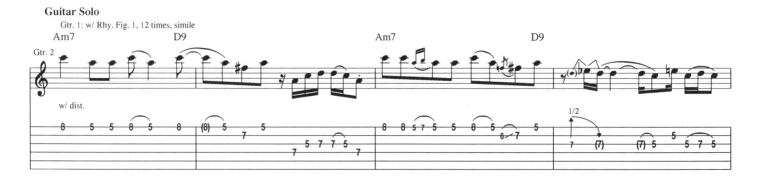

w/ dist.

Am7   D9   Am7   D9

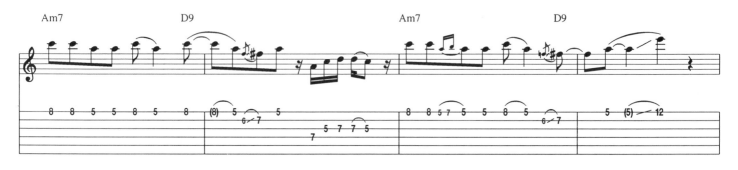

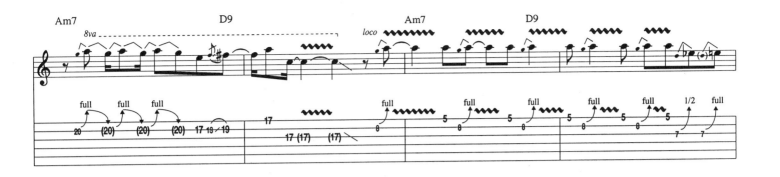

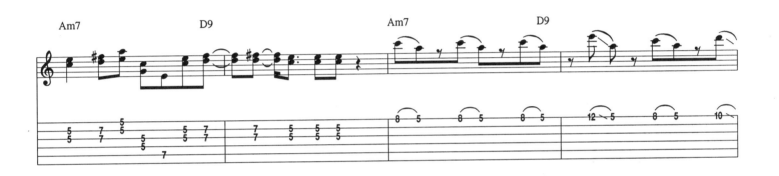

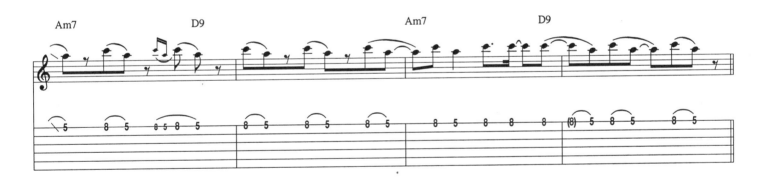

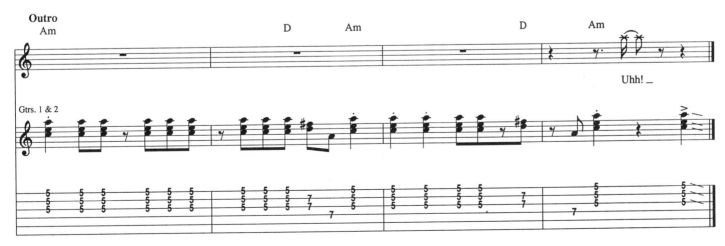

Persuasion

Words and Music by Gregg Rolie

* Key signature denotes F Dorian.

Samba Pa Ti

Words and Music by Carlos Santana

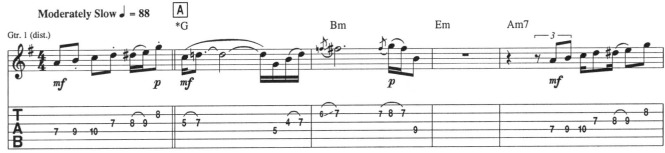

* Chord symbols reflect overall tonality.

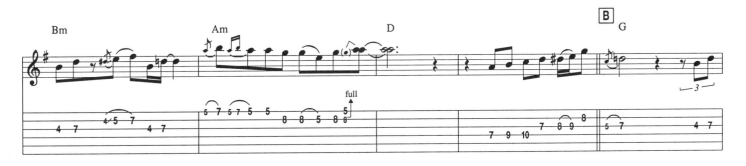

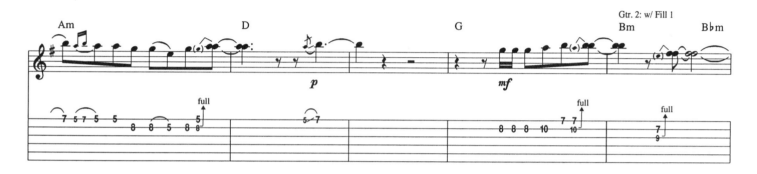

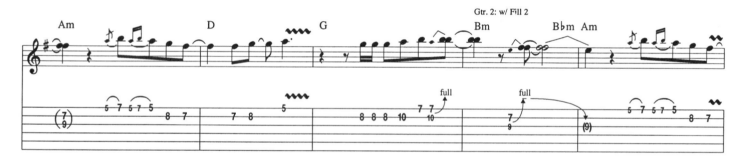

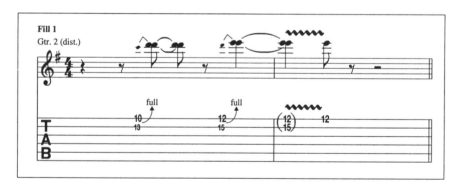

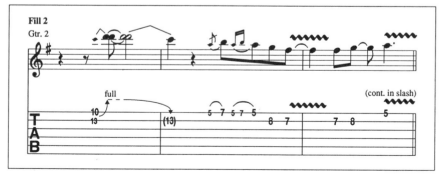

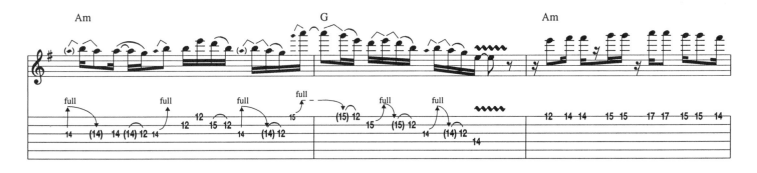

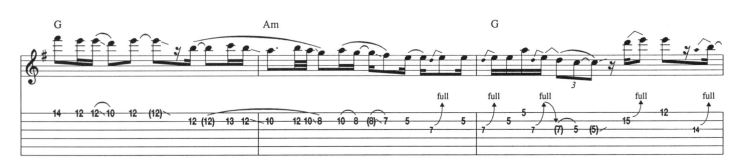

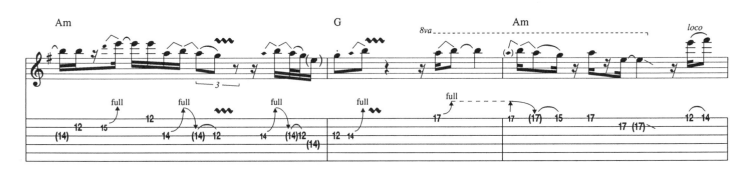

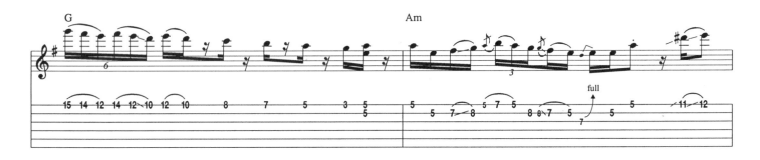

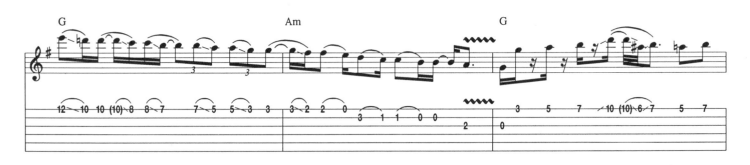

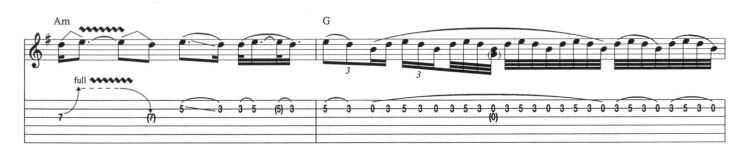

Singing Winds, Crying Beasts

Words and Music by Michael Carabello

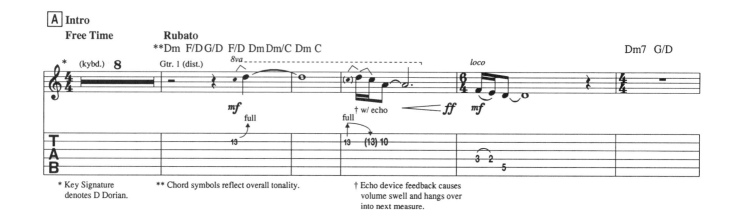

* Key Signature
denotes D Dorian.

** Chord symbols reflect overall tonality.

† Echo device feedback causes
volume swell and hangs over
into next measure.

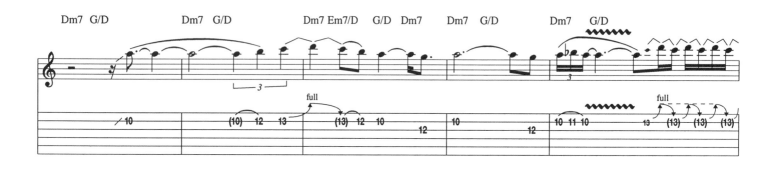

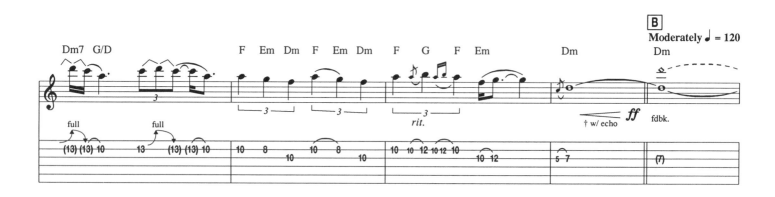

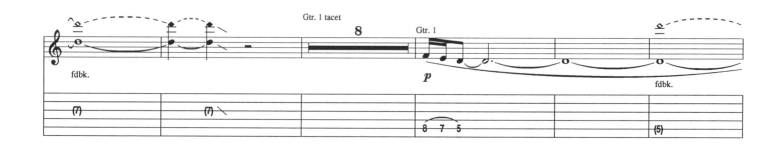

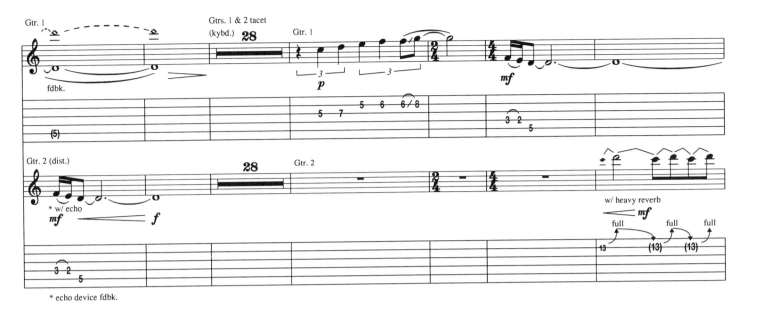

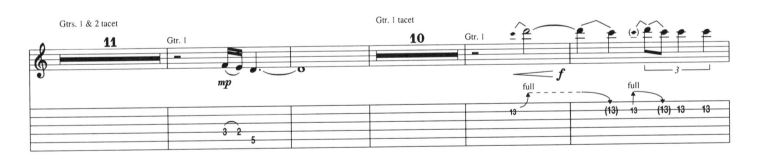

Fade into "Black Magic Woman"

Se A Cabo

Words and Music by Jose Areas

Song of the Wind

Music by Gregg Rolie, Neal Schon and Carlos Santana

* Chord symbols implied by organ & bass.

Soul Sacrifice

Words and Music by Carlos Santana

Toussaint L'Overture

Words and Music by Michael Shrieve, Gregg Rolie and Michael Carabello

Va - mo-nos, ne - gra, a bai - lar _____ mi Gua - guan - co.

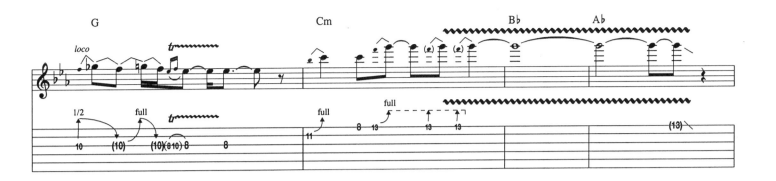

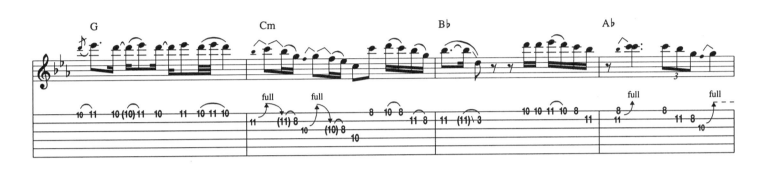

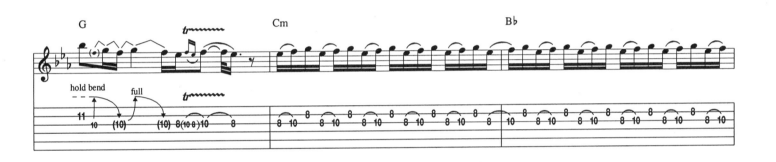

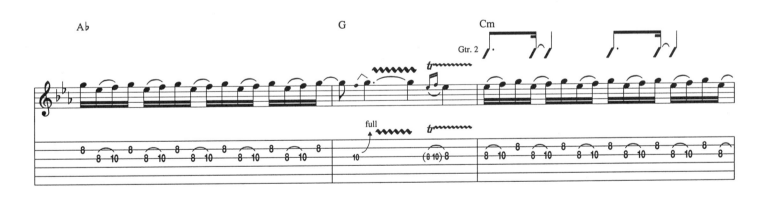

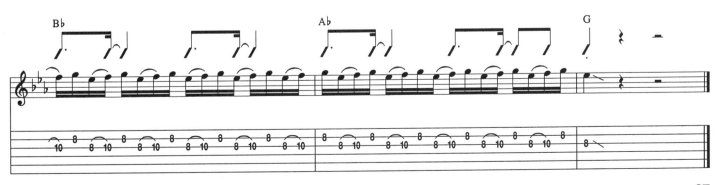

Winning

Words and Music by Russ Ballard

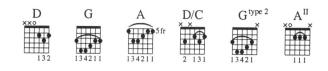

* Chord symbols derived from kybd.

(cont. in slash)

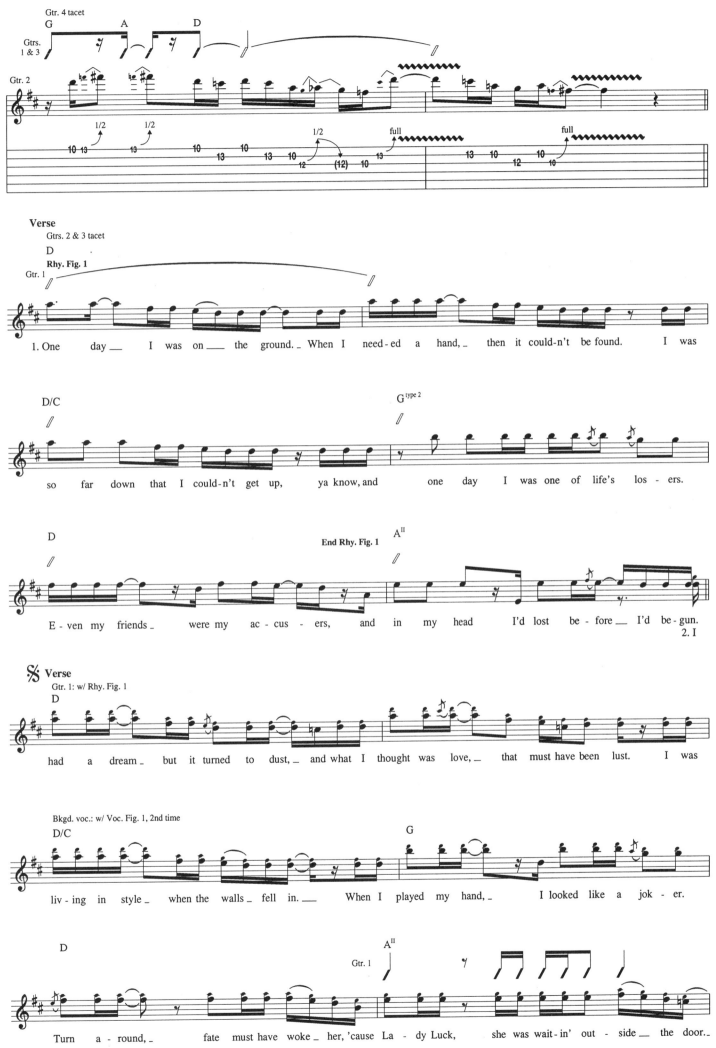

90

Gtr. 3: w/ Riff C, till fade
Gtr. 4: w/ Rhy. Fig. 3, simile, till fade

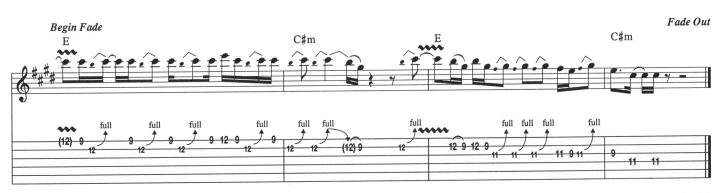

Guitar Notation Legend

Guitar Music can be notated three different ways: on a *musical staff*, in *tablature*, and in *rhythm slashes*.

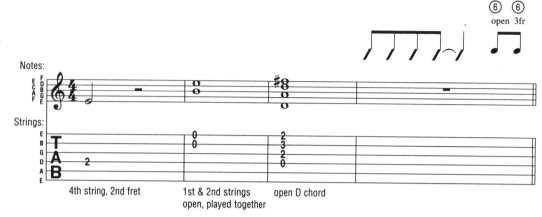

RHYTHM SLASHES are written above the staff. Strum chords in the rhythm indicated. Use the chord diagrams found at the top of the first page of the transcription for the appropriate chord voicings. Round noteheads indicate single notes.

THE MUSICAL STAFF shows pitches and rhythms and is divided by bar lines into measures. Pitches are named after the first seven letters of the alphabet.

TABLATURE graphically represents the guitar fingerboard. Each horizontal line represents a a string, and each number represents a fret.

Notes:

Strings:

4th string, 2nd fret

1st & 2nd strings open, played together

open D chord

Definitions for Special Guitar Notation

HALF-STEP BEND: Strike the note and bend up 1/2 step.

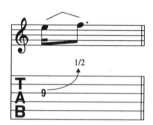

WHOLE-STEP BEND: Strike the note and bend up one step.

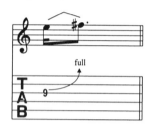

GRACE NOTE BEND: Strike the note and bend up as indicated. The first note does not take up any time.

SLIGHT (MICROTONE) BEND: Strike the note and bend up 1/4 step.

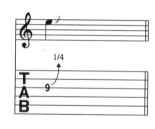

BEND AND RELEASE: Strike the note and bend up as indicated, then release back to the original note. Only the first note is struck.

PRE-BEND: Bend the note as indicated, then strike it.

PRE-BEND AND RELEASE: Bend the note as indicated. Strike it and release the bend back to the original note.

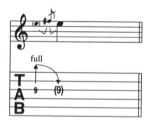

UNISON BEND: Strike the two notes simultaneously and bend the lower note up to the pitch of the higher.

VIBRATO: The string is vibrated by rapidly bending and releasing the note with the fretting hand.

WIDE VIBRATO: The pitch is varied to a greater degree by vibrating with the fretting hand.

HAMMER-ON: Strike the first (lower) note with one finger, then sound the higher note (on the same string) with another finger by fretting it without picking.

PULL-OFF: Place both fingers on the notes to be sounded. Strike the first note and without picking, pull the finger off to sound the second (lower) note.

LEGATO SLIDE: Strike the first note and then slide the same fret-hand finger up or down to the second note. The second note is not struck.

SHIFT SLIDE: Same as legato slide, except the second note is struck.

TRILL: Very rapidly alternate between the notes indicated by continuously hammering on and pulling off.

TAPPING: Hammer ("tap") the fret indicated with the pick-hand index or middle finger and pull off to the note fretted by the fret hand.

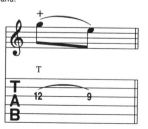

94

NATURAL HARMONIC: Strike the note while the fret-hand lightly touches the string directly over the fret indicated.

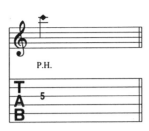

Harm.

PINCH HARMONIC: The note is fretted normally and a harmonic is produced by adding the edge of the thumb or the tip of the index finger of the pick hand to the normal pick attack.

P.H.

HARP HARMONIC: The note is fretted normally and a harmonic is produced by gently resting the pick hand's index finger directly above the indicated fret (in parentheses) while the pick hand's thumb or pick assists by plucking the appropriate string.

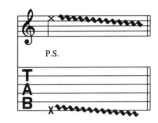

H.H.

PICK SCRAPE: The edge of the pick is rubbed down (or up) the string, producing a scratchy sound.

P.S.

MUFFLED STRINGS: A percussive sound is produced by laying the fret hand across the string(s) without depressing, and striking them with the pick hand.

PALM MUTING: The note is partially muted by the pick hand lightly touching the string(s) just before the bridge.

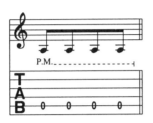

P.M.

RAKE: Drag the pick across the strings indicated with a single motion.

rake

TREMOLO PICKING: The note is picked as rapidly and continuously as possible.

ARPEGGIATE: Play the notes of the chord indicated by quickly rolling them from bottom to top.

VIBRATO BAR DIVE AND RETURN: The pitch of the note or chord is dropped a specified number of steps (in rhythm) then returned to the original pitch.

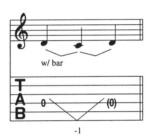

w/ bar

VIBRATO BAR SCOOP: Depress the bar just before striking the note, then quickly release the bar.

w/ bar

VIBRATO BAR DIP: Strike the note and then immediately drop a specified number of steps, then release back to the original pitch.

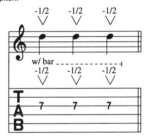

w/ bar

Additional Musical Definitions

(accent) • Accentuate note (play it louder)

(accent) • Accentuate note with great intensity

(staccato) • Play the note short

⊓ • Downstroke

∨ • Upstroke

D.S. al Coda • Go back to the sign (𝄋), then play until the measure marked "*To Coda*," then skip to the section labelled "*Coda*."

D.S. al Fine • Go back to the beginning of the song and play until the measure marked "*Fine*" (end).

Rhy. Fig. • Label used to recall a recurring accompaniment pattern (usually chordal).

Riff • Label used to recall composed, melodic lines (usually single notes) which recur.

Fill • Label used to identify a brief melodic figure which is to be inserted into the arrangement.

Rhy. Fill • A chordal version of a Fill.

tacet • Instrument is silent (drops out).

• Repeat measures between signs.

‖1. ‖2. • When a repeated section has different endings, play the first ending only the first time and the second ending only the second time.

NOTE: Tablature numbers in parentheses mean:
1. The note is being sustained over a system (note in standard notation is tied), or
2. The note is sustained, but a new articulation (such as a hammer-on, pull-off, slide or vibrato begins, or
3. The note is a barely audible "ghost" note (note in standard notation is also in parentheses).

RECORDED VERSIONS
The Best Note-For-Note Transcriptions Available

ALL BOOKS INCLUDE TABLATURE

00690002 Aerosmith – Big Ones $22.95	00694798 George Harrison Anthology $19.95	00694974 Queen – A Night At The Opera $19.95
00694909 Aerosmith – Get A Grip $19.95	00690068 Return of The Hellecasters $19.95	00694969 Queensryche – Selections from
00692015 Aerosmith's Greatest Hits $19.95	00692930 Jimi Hendrix – Are You Experienced? $19.95	"Operation: Mindcrime" $19.95
00660133 Aerosmith – Pump $19.95	00692931 Jimi Hendrix – Axis: Bold As Love $19.95	00694910 Rage Against The Machine $19.95
00694865 Alice In Chains – Dirt $19.95	00694944 Jimi Hendrix – Blues $24.95	00693910 Ratt – Invasion of Your Privacy $19.95
00660225 Alice In Chains – Facelift $19.95	00660192 The Jimi Hendrix – Concerts $24.95	00693911 Ratt – Out Of The Cellar $19.95
00694925 Alice In Chains – Jar Of Flies/Sap $19.95	00692932 Jimi Hendrix – Electric Ladyland $24.95	00690055 Red Hot Chili Peppers – Bloodsugarsexmagik .$19.95
00694932 Allman Brothers Band – Vol. 1 . . . .$24.95	00694923 Jimi Hendrix – The Experience	00690090 Red Hot Chili Peppers – One Hot Minute $22.95
00694933 Allman Brothers Band – Vol. 2 . . . .$24.95	Collection Boxed Set $75.00	00690027 Red Hot Chili Peppers – Out In L.A. $19.95
00694934 Allman Brothers Band – Vol. 3 . . . .$24.95	00660099 Jimi Hendrix – Radio One $24.95	00694968 Red Hot Chili Peppers – Selections
00694826 Anthrax – Attack Of The Killer B's $19.95	00694919 Jimi Hendrix – Stone Free $19.95	from "What Hits!?" $22.95
00694876 Chet Atkins – Contemporary Styles $19.95	00660024 Jimi Hendrix – Variations On A Theme:	00694892 Guitar Style Of Jerry Reed $19.95
00694877 Chet Atkins – Guitar For All Seasons $19.95	Red House $19.95	00694899 REM – Automatic For The People $19.95
00694918 The Randy Bachman Collection $22.95	00690017 Jimi Hendrix – Woodstock $24.95	00694898 REM – Out Of Time $19.95
00694929 Beatles: 1962-1966 . . . .$24.95	00690038 Gary Hoey – Best Of $19.95	00660060 Robbie Robertson $19.95
00694930 Beatles: 1967-1970 . . . .$24.95	00660029 Buddy Holly $19.95	00694959 Rockin' Country Guitar $19.95
00694880 Beatles – Abbey Road $19.95	00660200 John Lee Hooker – The Healer $19.95	00690014 Rolling Stones – Exile On Main Street $24.95
00694832 Beatles For Acoustic Guitar $19.95	00660169 John Lee Hooker – A Blues Legend $19.95	00694976 Rolling Stones – Some Girls $18.95
00660140 Beatles Guitar Book $19.95	00690054 Hootie & The Blowfish – Cracked Rear View .$19.95	00694897 Roots Of Country Guitar $19.95
00690044 Beatles – Live At The BBC $22.95	00694905 Howlin' Wolf $14.95	00694836 Richie Sambora – Stranger In This Town $19.95
00694891 Beatles – Revolver $19.95	00694850 Iron Maiden – Fear Of The Dark $19.95	00694805 Scorpions – Crazy World $19.95
00694914 Beatles – Rubber Soul $19.95	00694938 Elmore James – Master Electric Slide Guitar . .$14.95	00694916 Scorpions – Face The Heat $19.95
00694863 Beatles –	00694833 Billy Joel For Guitar $19.95	00694870 Seattle Scene $18.95
Sgt. Pepper's Lonely Hearts Club Band $19.95	00660147 Eric Johnson $19.95	00690076 Sex Pistols – Never The Bollocks,
00694931 Belly – Star $19.95	00694912 Eric Johnson – Ah Via Musicom $19.95	Here's The Sex Pistols $19.95
00694884 The Best of George Benson $19.95	00694911 Eric Johnson – Tones $19.95	00690041 Smithereens – Best Of $19.95
00692385 Chuck Berry $19.95	00694799 Robert Johnson – At The Crossroads $19.95	00694885 Spin Doctors – Pocket Full Of Kryptonite $19.95
00692200 Black Sabbath – We Sold Our Soul	00693185 Judas Priest – Vintage Hits $19.95	00694962 Spin Doctors – Turn It Upside Down $19.95
For Rock 'N' Roll $19.95	00660050 B. B. King $19.95	00694917 Spin Doctors – Up For Grabs $19.95
00694770 Jon Bon Jovi – Blaze Of Glory $19.95	00690019 King's X – Best Of $19.95	00694921 Steppenwolf, The Best Of $22.95
00690008 Bon Jovi – Cross Road $19.95	00694903 The Best Of Kiss $24.95	00694801 Rod Stewart, Best Of $22.95
00694871 Bon Jovi – Keep The Faith $19.95	00694903 Live – Throwing Copper $19.95	00694957 Rod Stewart – Unplugged...And Seated $22.95
00694775 Bon Jovi – Slippery When Wet $19.95	00690070 Live – Throwing Copper $19.95	00690021 Sting – Fields Of Gold $19.95
00690102 Bon Jovi – These Days $19.95	00694954 Lynyrd Skynyrd, New Best Of $19.95	00694824 Best Of James Taylor $16.95
00694935 Boston: Double Shot Of Boston $22.95	00694845 Yngwie Malmsteen – Fire And Ice $19.95	00694846 Testament – The Ritual $19.95
00694762 Cinderella – Heartbreak Station $19.95	00694756 Yngwie Malmsteen – Marching Out $19.95	00694887 Thin Lizzy – The Best Of Thin Lizzy $19.95
00692376 Cinderella – Long Cold Winter $19.95	00694755 Yngwie Malmsteen – Rising Force $19.95	00690030 Toad The Wet Sprocket $19.95
00692375 Cinderella – Night Songs $19.95	00660001 Yngwie Malmsteen's Rising Force – Odyssey . .$19.95	00694410 The Best of U2 . . . .$19.95
00694875 Eric Clapton – Boxed Set $75.00	00694757 Yngwie Malmsteen – Trilogy $19.95	00694411 U2 – The Joshua Tree $19.95
00692392 Eric Clapton – Crossroads Vol. 1 . . . .$22.95	00694956 Bob Marley – Legend $19.95	00690039 Steve Vai – Alien Love Secrets $24.95
00692393 Eric Clapton – Crossroads Vol. 2 . . . .$22.95	00690075 Bob Marley – Natural Mystic $19.95	00660137 Steve Vai – Passion & Warfare $24.95
00692394 Eric Clapton – Crossroads Vol. 3 . . . .$22.95	00694945 Bob Marley – Songs Of Freedom $24.95	00694904 Vai – Sex and Religion $24.95
00690010 Eric Clapton – From The Cradle $19.95	00690020 Meat Loaf – Bat Out Of Hell I & II $22.95	00690023 Jimmy Vaughan – Strange Pleasures $19.95
00660139 Eric Clapton – Journeyman $19.95	00694952 Megadeth – Countdown To Extinction $19.95	00690024 Stevie Ray Vaughan –
00694869 Eric Clapton – Unplugged $19.95	00694951 Megadeth – Rust In Peace $22.95	Couldn't Stand The Weather $19.95
00692391 The Best of Eric Clapton $19.95	00694953 Megadeth – Selections From "Peace Sells...	00694879 Stevie Ray Vaughan –In The Beginning $19.95
00694896 John Mayall/Eric Clapton – Bluesbreakers . . .$19.95	But Who's Buying?" &	00660136 Stevie Ray Vaughan – In Step $19.95
00694873 Eric Clapton – Timepieces $19.95	"So Far, So Good...So What!" $22.95	00660058 Stevie Ray Vaughan –
00694837 Albert Collins –	00690011 Megadeath – Youthanasia $19.95	Lightnin' Blues 1983 – 1987 . . . .$24.95
The Complete Imperial Recordings $19.95	00694868 Gary Moore – After Hours $19.95	00690036 Stevie Ray Vaughan – Live Alive $24.95
00694862 Contemporary Country Guitar $18.95	00694849 Gary Moore – The Early Years $19.95	00694835 Stevie Ray Vaughan – The Sky Is Crying $19.95
00660127 Alice Cooper – Trash $19.95	00694802 Gary Moore – Still Got The Blues $19.95	00690015 Stevie Ray Vaughan – Texas Flood $19.95
00694941 Crash Test Dummies – God Shuffled His Feet .$19.95	00690103 Alanis Morissette – Jagged Little Pill $19.95	00690025 Stevie Ray Vaughan – Soul To Soul $19.95
00694840 Cream – Disraeli Gears $19.95	00694958 Mountain, Best Of $19.95	00694776 Vaughan Brothers – Family Style $19.95
00690007 Danzig 4 . . . .$19.95	00694895 Nirvana – Bleach $19.95	00660196 Vixen – Rev It Up $19.95
00694844 Def Leppard – Adrenalize $19.95	00694913 Nirvana – In Utero $19.95	00694789 Muddy Waters – Deep Blues $24.95
00660186 Alex De Grassi Guitar Collection $19.95	00694901 Nirvana – Incesticide $19.95	00690071 Weezer $19.95
00694831 Derek And The Dominos – Layla	00694883 Nirvana – Nevermind $19.95	00694888 Windham Hill Guitar Sampler $18.95
& Other Assorted Love Songs $19.95	00690026 Nirvana – Unplugged In New York $19.95	
00660175 Dio – Lock Up The Wolves $19.95	00694847 Best Of Ozzy Osbourne $22.95	
00660178 Willie Dixon $24.95	00694830 Ozzy Osbourne – No More Tears $19.95	*Prices and availability subject to change without notice.*
00694920 Best of Free $18.95	00694855 Pearl Jam – Ten $19.95	*Some products may not be available outside the U.S.A.*
00690089 Foo Fighters $19.95	00693800 Pink Floyd – Early Classics $19.95	FOR MORE INFORMATION, SEE YOUR LOCAL MUSIC DEALER,
00690042 Robben Ford Blues Collection $19.95	00693864 Police, The Best Of $18.95	OR WRITE TO:
00694894 Frank Gambale – The Great Explorers $19.95	00694967 Police – Message In A Box Boxed Set $70.00	
00694807 Danny Gatton – 88 Elmira St $19.95	00692535 Elvis Presley $18.95	
00694848 Genuine Rockabilly Guitar Hits $19.95	00690032 Elvis Presley – The Sun Sessions $22.95	
	00694975 Queen – Classic $24.95	

0196